GW00645030

CAPE TOWN

CITY GUIDE *for* DESIGN LOVERS

The Travel Colours City Guides are for design-loving travellers who like to explore the trendiest places in each city, for travellers who see themselves as trendsetters. Each City Guide features a curated selection of the best places to "sleep, eat, drink, shop and explore", all of which have been personally tried and tested.

Edition TWO

EDITOR IN CHIEF
STEFANIE FRIESE

PHOTOGRAPHY BY
CLAIRE GUNN, STEFANIE FRIESE

WORDS BY
HANNI HEINRICH

PUBLISHED BY
FRIESE MEDIA GMBH, 2019
2ND EDITION - OCTOBER 2019

PRINTED AND BOUND BY
HARTMANNDRUCK & MEDIEN GMBH IN
GERMANY ON FSC CERTIFIED UNCOATED
PAPER

ISBN   978-3-9821148-4-2

SAY HELLO
GENERAL ENQUIRIES: hello@travelcolours.de
DISTRIBUTION: sales@travelcolours.de

MORE CITY GUIDES AVAILABLE AT
www.travelcolours.guide

WE TAKE CARE

OF YOU AND OF MOTHER EARTH

We work closely with a family-run printing company that has been printing climate-neutral for years together with ClimatePartner. All our books are printed exclusively on FSC-certified paper.

STEFANIE FRIESE

It has to be nice and a bit different. The desire for lifestyle and design is always guaranteed. As the founder of Travel Colours, Stefanie is always in search of the most beautiful places.

CLAIRE GUNN

As a former chef, Claire loves to show what's happening behind the scenes to create the magic on the plates. Today, you can find her shooting the theatre in Cape Town's exciting kitchens as widely-respected photographer.

HANNI HEINRICH

As a writer, Hanni is inspired by people, human behaviour and beaches. Her favourite body lotion is sun blocker factor 50. Born in Merseburg, Germany, she is currently based in Cape Town.

LOVE LETTER

Crowned by the magnificent Table Mountain and surrounded by superb beaches, there is nothing quite like Cape Town. Offering a blend of cultures, history, an exquisite wine and food scene, stunning nature and some of the most exciting wildlife in the world, Cape Town is also establishing itself internationally as a hub for art and design.

This Cape Town guide provides a curated selection of the locals' favourite places to "sleep, eat, drink, shop and explore". From serious coffee culture, farm markets and internationally acclaimed gourmet restaurants and award-winning wine estates to one of the oldest fishing villages along the West Coast, this guide will lead you away from the tourist hubs to some of Cape Town's hidden gems.

Stefanie Friese

EDITOR IN CHIEF

SLEEP

CAPE VIEW CLIFTON

UNINTERRUPTED VIEWS

Rumour has it that uninterrupted views of Cape Town's iconic Clifton and Camps Bay coastline have healing properties. Providing an opportunity to find this out, Cape View Clifton offers seven elegantly appointed, expansive suites. All of them are easygoing and elegant, decorated in calm-inducing hues and peppered with subtle colonial touches and modern artworks.

Located on the slopes of Lions Head, this luxury accommodation offers a balance between privacy and access to Cape Town's top restaurants and beaches; perfect for exploring all Cape Town's beauty and attractions. And, if the wind might blow a bit too much, the indoor fitness centre provides a healthy start to the sunny days of the Mother City.

232 Kloof Rd, Clifton, Cape Town, 8005
www.capeviewclifton.co.za

THE SILO HOTEL

CONTEMPORARY LUXURY HOTEL

Once a grain silo, now an extraordinary luxury hotel situated at Cape Town's V&A Waterfront. The building has retained the original steel columns that run every four metres throughout the hotel. Twenty-eight individually designed rooms are constructed across six floors. In the lobby, a showpiece chandelier by Haldane Martin hangs among original grain hoppers, while an original machine head rises through the floor of the "Willaston Bar". The Silo Hotel sets a new standard for accommodation, as it is not only brimming with over 300 pieces of contemporary African art, but also offers the finest cuisine and fantastic views. The experience at The Silo Hotel is focused on the art and culture of Cape Town.

Silo Square, V & A Waterfront, Cape Town, 8001
www.theroyalportfolio.com/thesilo

GORGEOUS GEORGE

INDUSTRIAL CHIC DESIGN HOTEL

Gorgeous George is the first Design Hotel™ in Cape Town's historic downtown. In the heart of the Mother City, between St. George's Mall and the popular Green Market Square, this hotel is a melting pot of Cape Town's unique cultural diversity and history. Guests are immersed in South Africa's dynamic design scene throughout the 32 rooms and communal spaces including Gigi Rooftop, the hotel's flagship restaurant, pool and bar. The Gorgeous George is surrounded by the Company's Garden and is only a one-kilometre walk to the V&A Waterfront. The 32 luxury rooms range from studios to one- and two-bedroom suites featuring industrial tones of raw, exposed concrete and steelwork, blended with modern Victorian design elements.

118 St Georges Mall, Cape Town, 8000

www.gorgeousgeorge.co.za

LA GRENADINE

OASIS OF TRANQUILITY

Tucked away almost invisible, this elegant guesthouse is situated close to bustling Kloof Street in the centre of Cape Town. The wooden doors are the gateway to a different world. As soon as one opens and enters, a magic tale happens and it is difficult to believe that you are still in Cape Town's busy centre. The garden of La Grenadine Petite Hotel offers antique tables and chairs under old pomegranate, guava, avocado and olive trees. The French owners Melodie and Maxime fell in love with Cape Town and decided to combine vintage with modern designer elements. It worked, with five beautiful en-suite bedrooms in a unique mix of industrial and French Provençal styles are waiting in the picturesque garden, behind magical wooden doors.

15 Park Rd, Gardens, Cape Town, 8001
www.lagrenadine.co.za

POD

MODERN DESIGN & ARCHITECTURE

This exclusive accommodation on the shores of Camps Bay boasts 17 rooms with views of the sea and mountain. Quiet, yet still close to the bustling Main Road of Camps Bay, this boutique hotel presents modern design, clean lines and green architecture with a hint of the simplicity of a seaside holiday. At POD Camps Bay, each room is unique and distinctive, just like the individuals who choose to stay here. POD's guests will love the attention to detail, including architect Greg Scott's eco features such as the sustainable water supply and energy-saving lighting and insulation. If one is lucky, celebrities can be spotted here, relaxing and enjoying Cape Town's abundance of beautiful views.

3 Argyle St, Camps Bay, Cape Town, 8005
www.pod.co.za

PERFECT HIDEAWAYS

UNIQUE HOLIDAY HOUSES

Perfect Hideaways has a bouquet of farms, villas and elegant accommodation, each unique and individual. The idea behind it is to find the perfect tailor-made getaway that promises a truly unforgettable escape. Perfect Hideaways appeals to every sense and offers a selection for every taste imaginable. With over 200 extraordinary holiday escapes on its books, Perfect Hideaways has shown love to unusual destinations, quaint villages and interesting properties, such as "Bobbejaansberg", an exclusive stone-built dream house with a copper bathtub, sitting in splendid isolation in Klein Karoo. Each location is carefully sourced, each property is truly stylish, and the thoughtfully-appointed interiors all with luxury details ensure comfort and an unforgettable experience.

www.perfecthideaways.co.za

CLIFTON BUNGALOW 47

PERFECT BEACH HIDEAWAY

Sandy feet and salty kisses, legs up on the sofa and ocean breezes all feature at Clifton 47. Situated at one of Cape Town's best beaches, Clifton 4th beach, this mesmerising bungalow offers everything that elegant beach lovers wouldn't want to miss. Only 42 steps away from the white sands, large glass sliders in every room let the sunshine in, while nothing inside steals away the breathtaking view. Modern touches to this otherwise typical beach bungalow give it a clean, contemporary feel, which, combined with the exceptional setting, creates a rather fabulous effect.

Clifton, Cape Town
www.perfecthideaways.co.za

LEMURIA

MODERN HOLIDAY HOUSE

At first sight this place might look like a simple stone cottage hidden on the beach at Bettys Bay. But this is a modern holiday house and shows contemporary design with large spaces, a dramatic black backdrop offset with bright pinks, blues and golds. Lemuria is made for family holidays. What counts: forgetting time and relaxing. At the center is the living area with breathtaking views across the ever-changing ocean. On hot days the tree in the courtyard offers welcome shade and a swimming pool caters for a cooling splash. Directly in front of the house is a nesting sanctuary for endangered Black Oyster Catchers; both bird-lovers and children will love to watch the new hatchlings.

Betty's Bay
www.perfecthideaways.co.za

ICARIA

DESIGN LOVER'S DREAM

Part of the Perfect Hideaways group, Icaria House in Bantry Bay is located on the steep mountain slopes of Cape Town's iconic Atlantic Seaboard. Not only blessed with breathtaking views across the sea and towards the mountain, Icaria is also full of surprises: this perfect hideaway is located inside the Table Mountain National Reserve and the entire southern edge of Icaria blends into this floral kingdom of fynbos-covered nature. Fantastic for serendipitous enjoyment of tranquillity.

Bantry Bay, Cape Town
www.perfecthideaways.co.za

EAT

WITH COFFEE

HEMELHUIJS

SOPHISTICATED OASIS

Being in heaven must have been Hemelhuijs' motto. When entering, the world changes into a jewel-coloured place. With its ever-changing interior space and displays of fresh flowers and object trofée, this restaurant is a small oasis in the heart of Cape Town, offering an escape from the hustle and bustle of the city centre. The menu changes seasonally, featuring local and international delicacies presented in a simple, attentive but relaxed way. Since opening in October 2010, the restaurant has invited everyone to enjoy and dream while indulging in crafted juices, artisan cocktails and, of course, dishes made with love. Hemelhuijs also boasts its own homeware range, which guests can experience during everyday service or take home.

71 Waterkant St, City Centre, Cape Town, 8001
www.hemelhuijs.co.za

STRANGERS CLUB

INTIMATE LIFESTYLE CAFÉ

This hidden gem in Greenpoint has quickly become a popular peaceful and quiet escape from city life, paired with healthy meals and drinks. The Strangers Club shares its property with Out of this World, a décor and furniture store for authentic tribal art. The atmosphere is relaxed with outdoor seating area only and casual wood benches. On the small delightful menu, everything is healthy and made fresh daily. Some of the favourites include turmeric and matcha lattes, nutty smoothie bowls topped with fruit, granola and goji berries, as well as the avocado sandwich. The Strangers Club is a super sweet and intimate spot where you can happily sit and work alone or meet up with friends.

1 Braemar Rd, Green Point, Cape Town, 8005
no website

LOADING BAY

FASHION, FOOD AND DESIGN SPOT

Loading Bay has been mentioned several times in various magazines as one of the top fashion, food and design spots to visit in Cape Town. Located in the De Waterkant area, Loading Bay features a clean glass facade that makes it light and bright. It feels laid-back and casual, with an eye for practical and tangible application to one's everyday life. The clothing, much like its food and skincare products, features a notable connection to source, and how it relates to each individual's needs. The menu's focus is seasonal and precise and offers enough variety for all tastes. It is all about source from grass-fed pasture-raised meat, organic fruit and vegetables and ethically caught fish. Your appetite will certainly be satisfied.

30 Hudson St, De Waterkant, Cape Town, 8001
www.loadingbay.co.za

CLARKE'S

FASHIONABLE COFFEE PLACE

For herbivores and carnivores, this is a good place to be. Whether it's to enjoy hash eggs with toasted cauliflower for brunch, or Parmentier potatoes, two poached eggs, asparagus and sauce hollandaise for early dinner, this place is heaven for hipsters. While coffee lovers, wine and beer drinkers, gin fans and simple water drinkers philosophise, time flies and it can get quite busy at peak times. Loud laughter only adds to the sparkling party ambience created by fashionable and stylish customers who are easygoing and quick to flash a friendly smile.

133 Bree St, Cape Town City Centre, Cape Town, 8001
www.clarkesdining.co.za

MRKT

LOCALLY SOURCED PRODUCTS

MRKT, pronounced "market", is a newly established cafe found in Cape Town's foreshore district, open to guests and residents of The Onyx, and the public. Located on The Onyx's ground floor, this establishment serves a selection of wholesome breakfast and lunch items, harvest-inspired buffet offerings and simple but flavourful on-the-go meals. MRKT is also home to a barista station where brewed coffees are skillfully prepared. In addition, handcrafted bread and pastries are created in an open-plan bakery, emitting the most comforting aromas. The 110-seater establishment also includes a number of areas where patrons can sit for extended periods, working and collaborating while enjoying coffee, a bite to eat and views of the city.

57 Heerengracht St, Cape Town, 8005
www.newmarkhotels.com/places/in-house/mrkt/

LIVE BAIT

FRESHLY CAUGHT FISH

While showing off some of Cape Town's most magnificent views from Muizenberg and Kalk Bay harbour, Live Bait prides itself on providing guests with a family-friendly and comfortable dining experience. The seafood restaurant in Muizenberg is located at the famous surfer's corner near the beach where Agatha Christie once surfed on her board, "Fred".

In Kalk Bay, just a few kilometres further up the coastline, the second Live Bait branch lures hungry visitors with its freshly caught fish. This restaurant is a definite hotspot, especially for locals who love lazy Sunday lunches here while watching seagulls and the fishing boats that supply the restaurant with the daily catch.

www.livebait.co.za

LA PARADA AT
V&A WATERFRONT

CONTEMPORARY TAPAS

La Parada! The sound makes one feel happy and ready to get out and play. This eatery at the V&A Waterfront is the perfect location to enjoy cool cocktails or fine dining. The contemporary tapas menu can be appreciated in the Spanish-inspired lounge area while breathing the Atlantic sea breeze. Popular dishes are prawn croquettes, but there are also more robust offerings like crispy pork belly or the grilled cheese with ham and truffle on the menu. La Parada caters for every level of appetite and provides a sense of camaraderie and fun. La Parada V&A Waterfront joins its sister eateries at Constantia Nek and Bree Street.

1 Dock Rd, V & A Waterfront, Cape Town, 8001
www.laparada.co.za

THE YARD

FINE-DINING, DELI & CONCEPT STORE

The Yard Restaurant mindfully pairs the flavours of East and West, offering a re-imagined South African dining experience. Whether enjoying any of the freshly-prepared breakfasts, nutritious lunches or delectable dinners, each meal pays homage to Mediterranean, Middle Eastern, Oriental and Indian influences. The design of this modern space is urban-industrial chic, with sleek marble countertops, concrete walls decorated with altering contemporary art and an open kitchen. Situated directly opposite the Zeitz Museum of Contemporary Art Africa in the Waterfronts Silo District, The Yard is named for the surrounding dockyards located within view of the picturesque tugboat moorings and the waters of Cape Town harbour.

Ground Floor, Silo 4, Silo District, Cape Town, 8001
www.theyardatsilo.co.za

UNFRAMED ICE CREAM

ICE CREAM ARTISTRY

In the heart of the Mother City, surrounded by restaurants and coffee shops, this little gem offers cool delicacies on a hot summer's day, and the best part is that it's healthy too. The artisanal ice-cream is made with carefully selected ingredients and offers dairy-based, fruit-based sorbets and nut-based vegan options. Those who want to add toppings can choose from a selection of superfoods. The flavours are classic with a twist, 10 flavours are on display daily, rotating according to the season, inspiration and supply. For all vegans, at least two sorbets and three vegan options are offered at all times.

45C Kloof St, Gardens, Cape Town, 8001
www.unframed.co.za

EAT

WITH WINE

LA TÊTE

NOSE-TO-TAIL

Two brothers fulfilled their dream by opening this restaurant in November 2016. Changing London for Cape Town, the duo decided that La Tête would be a so-called farm-to-fork restaurant, with emphasis on traceability and sustainable farming practices for a wide range of menu options. They change the menu daily depending on what's fresh and available from a small number of carefully-chosen suppliers. There is no wrong choice when eating here: grilled aubergine and parsley or sweetbreads, peas and bacon or grilled ox heart, chips and ketchup. La Tête embraces innovation and a rather unconventional menu, using all parts of all ingredients. The décor is minimalistic. The space is simple, so no one is distracted. La Tête is all about a holistic eating philosophy.

17 Bree St, Cape Town City Centre, Cape Town, 8000
www.latete.co.za

THE STACK

NOT JUST A PRIVATE MEMBERS CLUB

Cosy, posh, sociable and in-vouge in the same breath. The Stack is a fashionable brasserie and bar downstairs with a private members' club upstairs, housed in the historic Leinster Hall in Gardens.

The a la carte menu at the bistro offers a range of delicious, classic bistro and exquisite French fare. The fries are crispy and the sirloin perfectly cooked. The Béarnaise is rich and the classic crème brûlée perfect for a sweet ending.

As a bar and a brasserie, the colourful bar offers remarkable long drinks while waiting to be seated next door. The brasserie favours a more neutral colour palette, shining sophisticated, stylish and elegant at once: perfect for a fancy date night or dinner with the in-laws.

7 Weltevreden St, Gardens, Cape Town, 8001
www.thestack.co.za

SEABREEZE FISH & SHELL

FINEST FRESH FISH

The ocean is the theme of this seafood restaurant. Decorated in calming shades of blue and stripped back wood, it's twice-daily happy hours kick off with oysters from three different sources: Knysna on the East Coast, Saldanha on the West Coast and Lüderitz from Namibia. Tasting each is an experience in merroir – the taste of the sea – and are served with SeaBreeze's home-made Mignonette: a red wine and shallot vinaigrette with all the usual accompaniments. SeaBreeze also offers various local fish, prawns or shellfish sourced daily. Served in delicious sauces or combined with salads, pasta, local vegetables or hand-cut fries, however, the most popular dish is the classic hake and chips, battered gloriously golden and airy.

213 Bree St, Cape Town City Centre, Cape Town, 8000
www.seabreezecapetown.co.za

RIVERINE RABBIT

CONSCIOUS FINE DINING EXPERIENCE

Inspired by an indigenous animal found in the Karoo – a South African rock desert – that is facing extinction, the riverine rabbit is the name of Ash Heeger's and Mandy van der Berg's restaurant. With a focus on sustainability, locally sourced seasonal produce, and mindful preparation of food, Riverine Rabbit offers a three-course menu and a five-course tasting menu, as well as a seven-course dégustation paired with a selection of wines. For the very curious food lovers, one can opt for the intimate chef's table experience – providing a look into the kitchen and time to chat with Chef Ash. Ash Heeger was one of 24 chefs handpicked from around the world to compete in the Netflix production *The Final Table*.

81 Church St, Cape Town, 8000
www.riverinerabbit.com

THE TEST KITCHEN

EXTRAORDINARY FINE DINING

The Test Kitchen is not just a restaurant: it's an experience. At this intimate space, star chef Luke Dale-Roberts applies his expert technique and passion for true flavour in the creation of the finest, most creative dishes. The journey starts in the Dark Room through the world of foods, from Europe to Peru to Japan and back to South Africa. Only then does the tour continue in the Light Room, where guests enjoy the remainder of the beautifully-plated menu in a more formal setting. The open kitchen is a stage where chefs perform artistic moves, often intuiting what is needed without words. Each of the 21 courses of the tasting menu is a taste sensation. Each plate has its own style, visually reflecting the flavours on the plate. Reservations open quarterly for three months in advance and are highly recommended.

The Old Biscuit Mill, 375 Albert Rd, Woodstock, Cape Town, 7915

www.thetestkitchen.co.za

CHEFS WAREHOUSE & CANTEEN

GOURMET LUNCHES AND TAPAS

This restaurant is famous for its tapas-for-two menu and has been extremely well received in Cape Town. Each day, after every service, the chefs get together to decide what they will serve the next day. So, be prepared to see a completely different menu every day, often based on what is available and seasonal. The set menu comprises eight courses to share and typically contains seafood dishes and vegetarian options, while the rest is made up of meat. The atmosphere is relaxed canteen-style. Bookings are not accepted, so come as early as possible.

92 Bree St, Cape Town, 8000
www.chefswarehouse.co.za

FYN

FINE DINING ON THE ROOFTOP

FYN is the Afrikaans word for "fine" and the beginning of the word "fynbos", South Africa's unique species of the Cape floral kingdom. FYN is fine dining. With its generously proportioned open-plan kitchen, this restaurant offers seasonal South African ingredients served in the Japanese kaiseki tradition. Diners can expect new items to be added to the menu almost weekly. With dishes such as rice smoked duck breast, fermented pear, liver crémeux; seasonal ingredients are expertly combined to produce unique flavours. At FYN, the eye is indulged too: the rooftop showcases unrivalled views of Lion's Head and Table Mountain.

5th Floor, 37 Parliament St, Cape Town, 8000
www.fynrestaurant.com

THE POT LUCK CLUB

EXCITING TASTE ADVENTURE

A glass lift whisks guests to the sixth floor of the Old Biscuit Mill: this rooftop space with a 360-degree view of Cape Town is the sister restaurant of The Test Kitchen. Here, star chef Dale-Roberts and head chef Jason Kosmas serve a more casual menu. Dishes are organised according to five flavours; salty, sour, sweet, umami and bitter to allow guests to try each sensation on its own as well as all the flavours as a whole experience. The menu is decidedly global, with a distinctive Asian flair and a strong focus on local produce with some signatures perennially featured. Dishes are designed to be passed around, shared and snacked upon, and the result is a decidedly down-to-earth atmosphere.

The Old Biscuit Mill, 375 Albert Rd, Woodstock, Cape Town, 7915

www.thepotluckclub.co.za

THE SHORTMARKET CLUB

FINE BISTRO-STYLE CUISINE

The Shortmarket Club has already become a stalwart on the city's fine dining scene. The menu features a modern interpretation of classic bistro-style cuisine, which has been extremely well received among locals. The stylish yet cosy interior has the look and feel of a members-only private club, making it a place to relax in a luxurious surrounding with beautifully-arranged dishes. One highlight is the open kitchen with a braai section, from where one is served meat dishes. In the main dining room, the centrepiece is a wall of framed paper butterflies made from old documents from Chef Wesley and Manager Simon's journeys and includes, architectural blueprints, photos and letters. Reservations are highly recommended.

88 Shortmarket St, Cape Town, 8000
www.theshortmarketclub.co.za

SALSIFY AT THE ROUNDHOUSE

FINE DINING AND SUPERB VIEW

This fine-dining eatery at The Roundhouse in Camps Bay is surrounded by leafy trees, hugged by the iconic Lion's Head. Salsify at the Roundhouse is a collaboration between two Cape Town fine dining connoisseurs: Luke Dale-Roberts and Ryan Cole. Together, they have changed the luxury dining scene in the city with their award-winning The Test Kitchen. The focus at Salsify is "root to leaf" dining with an emphasis on refined dining without pomp. Gourmands should be excited about the micro-seasons Cape Town experiences; and the produce that's only available for a few weeks at a time. Salsify is perfect at sunset when golden light streams through the trees onto the white tablecloths and Persian rugs.

The Roundhouse, Camps Bay, 8005
www.salsify.co.za

FOXCROFT

REFINED, BUT RELAXED DINING

"Prepared with great attention to detail. Showing sophisticated elegance, carefully or elegantly done", is the guiding principle of Foxcroft. The sister restaurant to La Colombe has quickly established itself as one of the best restaurants in Cape Town since its opening in 2016, and it is the perfect place if one is looking for a fine-dining experience that is casual, welcoming and carefully considered. Open for lunch and dinner, guests enjoy a four-course menu prepared by head chef and co-owner Glen Williams. Every ingredient is carefully selected for seasonality, quality and flavour before entering the kitchen at Foxcroft. Indeed, each dish that comes out of the open kitchen is beautifully crafted and presented on the most exquisite crockery.

High Constantia Centre, Groot Constantia Road, Constantia, 7806
www.foxcroft.co.za

CHEFS WAREHOUSE AT BEAU CONSTANTIA

ULTIMATE FOOD EXPERIENCE

Light. Style. Cuisine. This restaurant is a triangle of love for everyone who enjoys quality in all fields of life. Overlooking False Bay and the vineyards, the large windows allow the interior to be flooded with natural light and offer a picturesque view. The open kitchen provides a preview of all ingredients, which are transformed into edible art. Taste matters, so it's no wonder most of the ingredients are fresh from the local garden. The menu changes often, depending on the season. Eight different tapas dishes are provided over three courses, with bread or oysters as a starter as well as a dessert at an additional charge.

Constantia Main Rd, Glen Alpine, Constantia, 7806
www.beauconstantia.com

DRINK

THE ATHLETIC CLUB & SOCIAL

THE PLACE FOR SOCIALISING

A cosy venue for romantic dates and group gatherings, this three-storey bar and restaurant offers abundance – from light lunches and hearty dinners to classy party nights. Located on bustling Buitengracht Street, the Victorian building provides beautiful views of Table Mountain from the large veranda. The building dates back to the 1900s when it housed an underground speakeasy-style bar for athletes.

Today, The Athletic Club & Social serves a menu combining Greek, Mediterranean and Middle Eastern flavours including vegetarian and vegan options. The meat and fish dishes are sustainably and ethically sourced. The vintage-style wallpaper, antique sports equipment and photographs on the walls should be admired as one journeys through the space. Once the sun has set, vinyl DJs play soul-filled music.

35 Buitengracht St, CBD, Cape Town, 8001
www.theathletic.co.za

TJING TJING HOUSE

WHERE JAPAN MEETS SOUTH AFRICA

Cape Town loves innovative concepts and one fine example is Tjing Tjing House. It smelts Japan and South Africa, in the heart of Cape Town. Providing four distinctly different venues in one house, the journey starts at Tjing Tjing Torii on street level where, inspired by the multiple layers of old and modern Japan, casual Japanese food can be enjoyed. On the first floor awaits Tjing Tjing Momiji, a meditative restaurant, offering a traditional Japanese kaiseki dining experience. The third stop is the Tjing Tjing Rooftop Bar, well-known for its current indie and electronic music. The Japanese shrine-inspired red bar and a Tokyo and Kyoto photo wall refine the taste of bespoke cocktails, spirits, wine and otsumami.

165 Longmarket St, Cape Town City Centre, Cape Town, 8001
www.tjingtjing.co.za

THE GIN BAR

WHEN GIN MEETS CHOCOLATE

No one knows whether the location is a chocolatier, a gallery or a bar. It is a secret. But whether it is this or that, it doesn't matter because what everyone knows that this Victorian-style bar is an undercover gem in Cape Town's city centre, where insiders go once the sun has set. This is a dedicated gin bar comprising four main cocktails. The secret here is quality rather than quantity. Cleverly named Head, Heart, Soul and Ambition, the gins are refreshing, tasty and deliciously subtle in flavour. The Gin Bar has recently expanded into a larger main space and is open for lunch daily. It shares a charming courtyard with Honest Chocolate.

64A Wale St, Cape Town City Centre, Cape Town, 8000
www.theginbar.co.za

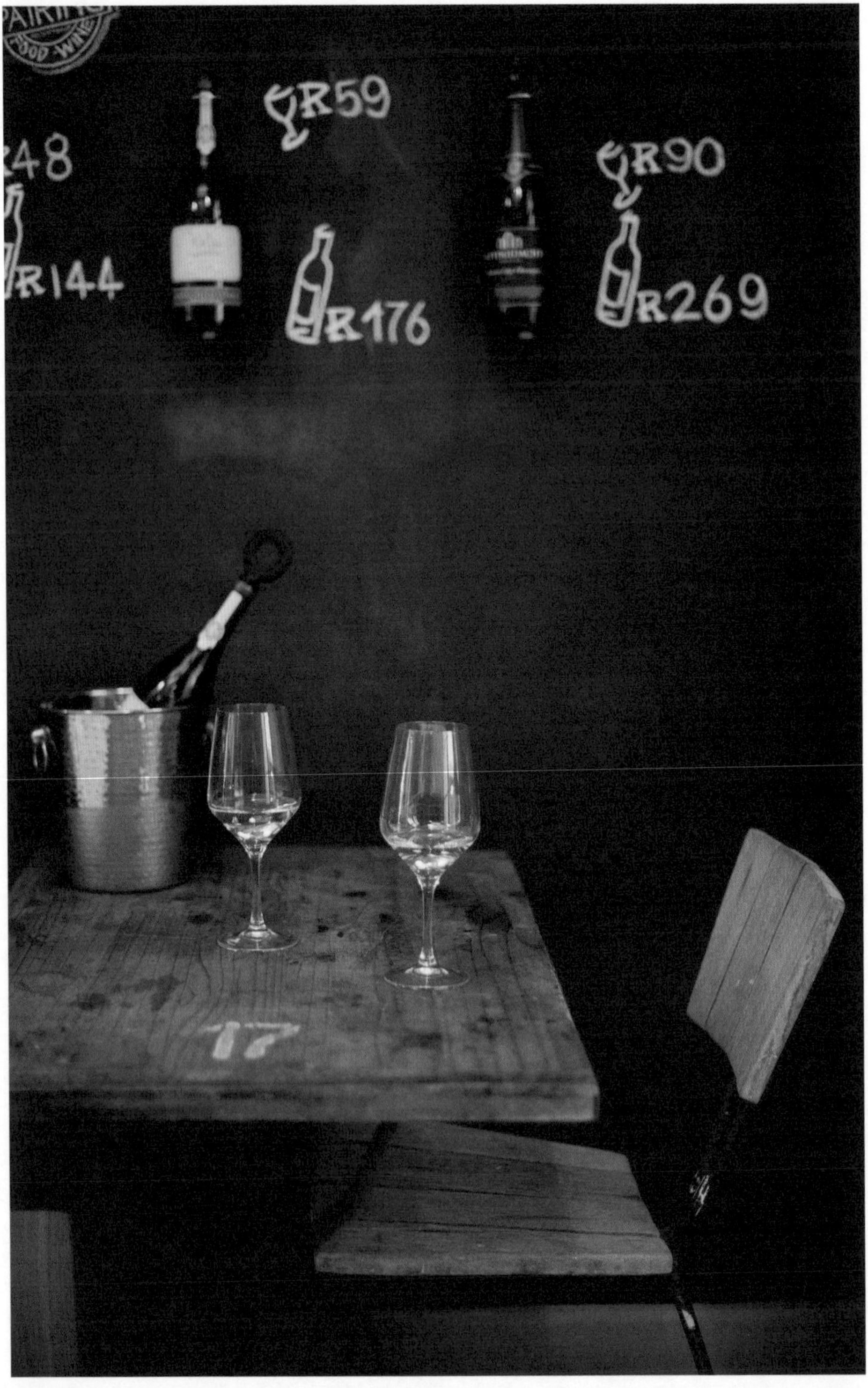

R59
R144
R176
R90
R269
17

OPEN WINE

AN ITALIAN CONCEPT

The name promises the programme, with an Italian twist. Openwine is an enoteca, a little palace of wine, where everyone can enjoy a glass (or two) of quality local wine. The space is divided into the kitchen, the lounge and the cellar. The kitchen area encourages guests to sniff, swirl and sip the juice of the grape, the lounge offers a comfortable setting with a TV and the cellar, the "heart of Openwine", comprises a floor-to-wall wine shelf filled with various bottles of red, white and bubbly, as well as a wall-mounted chalkboard with various wine bottles. Openwine offers snacks and a weekly-changing chalkboard menu offers four dishes each paired with a suggested wine.

72 Wale St, Cape Town City Centre, Cape Town, 8001

www.openwineza.co.za

PUBLIK WINE BAR

ARTISAN SOUTH AFRICAN WINES

Publik is a neighbourhood wine bar with a focus on the more unusual and interesting wines combined with good cheeses, charcuterie and snacks. All wines served are made with love from sustainably-farmed vineyards. Offering blind tastings, it opens ways to learn more about wine, especially lesser-known wines. Everything at Publik is dedicated to artisanal South African wines. The goal is to share the best wines with customers, either in the bar, via the online store, or through the trade distribution operation. Publik does not have a telephone, so reservations cannot be made. Instead, this bar focuses on talking to guests about – guess – wine.

11D Kloof Nek Rd, Gardens, Cape Town, 8001
www.publik.co.za

POWER & GLORY

A PLACE YOU WANT TO BE SEEN AT

This neighbourhood bar is heaven for hipsters. Patrons wearing skinny jeans, red lipstick, Doc Martens, or a combination only a Berlin fashion blogger knows by name, gather here to talk, read and drink. That's what makes the Power and the Glory a home-from-home for the regulars who hang out here. It's slightly shabby but chic, in such a nice casual way, very comfortable and totally unintimidating: the way they like things in Tamboerskloof. From morning until late, the Power and the Glory offers snacks, craft beers and local wines.

13D Kloof Nek Rd, Tamboerskloof, Cape Town, 8000
no website

SHOP

SANS COMMUNITY

ORGANIC GROCERY STORE

Sans belongs to a trio that is a community of conscious living. It provides a neighbourhood grocer and home goods store in Sea Point connecting local communities with farmers, makers and producers focusing on a holistic and mindful lifestyle. At the same time, Sans has expert baristas at the coffee shop, Paulines, and a team at the mothership, Loading Bay in the De Waterkant district. Sans strives to create awareness and shares in conversation that encourages engagement and interaction with our natural worlds. By connecting with the source, Sans wants to grow a collective understanding of where food, products and our everyday items are coming from and how that not only affects our health and wellbeing, but our planet as well.

277 Main Rd, Sea Point, Cape Town, 8005
www.sanscommunity.com

DEAR RAE

MODERN, FEMININE AESTHETIC

Dear Rae is a proudly South African jewellery company, priding itself on working in solid metals, such as brass, silver and gold. It also provides a custom-design service for clients looking to have something special made including custom engagement rings. Dear Rae works with semi-precious stones and has added unique colour diamonds to its standard collections. Each piece is designed and made by Karin and her hand-selected manufacturers at her Cape Town-based studio. Drawing on inspirations from her diverse South African and German familial heritage, Karin was inspired to launch Dear Rae in 2010. Her passion for empowering and employing local South Africans has been a driving force in the business.

164 Bree St, Cape Town City Centre, Cape Town, 8001

www.dearae.co.za

MAISON MARA & BASTILLE

EXCLUSIVE MULTI-BRAND STORE

For their concept store, Kelly Withey and Sylvain Pierre carefully handpick the latest designs from international fashion labels that are already suited to their customer's lifestyle. Maison Mara & Bastille bring some of the finest womenswear, menswear and accessories to the Mother City. Brands such as Ganni, Comme de Garçons, A.P.C & Veja can be found here. And so a touch of Paris breezes into Cape Town's colourful De Waterkant district in a building that dates back to the 1800s and has retained much of its heritage. One of the highlights is the marble bathroom on the 2nd floor featuring Malin+Goetz. The antique sink and shower are the perfect place to display beauty products and perfumes.

5 Jarvis St, De Waterkant, Cape Town, 8001

www.maisonmara.co.za

SOUTHERN GUILD

HIGH-END DESIGN

South Africa's premier design gallery provides a platform to showcase the very best of South African design from the most respected designers and artists in the country. Exhibiting locally and at leading design fairs around the world, the annual collection strives to progress, stimulate and promote the industry. In 2011, it became the first African gallery to present at Design Miami, and in 2015, it was the first to be featured at Christie's London's annual design auction. Today, the gallery exhibits regularly at Design Miami in Basel and the US, at Design Days Dubai and the Collective Design Fair in New York, resulting in sales to leading architects, top collectors and respected museums.

Silo 5, Unit 5B, South Arm Road, Silo District, Cape Town, 8001
www.southernguild.co.za

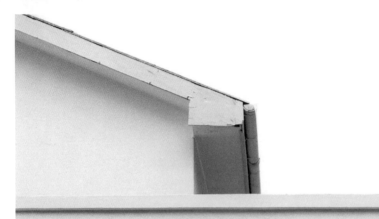

CHAPEL GOODS

HANDMADE LEATHER PRODUCTS

Caleb Pedersen began with Chapel in 2009, when riding bikes around Cape Town started to become more popular. At that time, Caleb needed a fashionable backpack into which he could fit in everything that needed for a full day. Since then, they have been making bags at their studio in Woodstock, from the best locally-sourced canvas and leather suppliers. Meanwhile, the bags have become a popular fashion accessory and Chapel offers a wide selection of finest leather goods, which are 100% made in Woodstock. You can find them at four locations in Cape Town. The picture was taken at their store on Kloof Street.

99C Kloof St, Gardens, Cape Town, 8001
www.chapelgoods.co.za

CLEMENTINA CERAMICS

HANDCRAFTED & UNIQUE

The Clementina Ceramics studio offers functional art for the dinner table, as well as architectural wall tiles. All items are handcrafted and individually painted and glazed. Vibrant colours reflect the light of Africa, bringing a sense of wellbeing to the human spirit. Each piece offers the user a sense of life's meaning. Designer and maker Clementina van der Walt is inspired by the African rural and urban landscapes. The ceramics made in this studio form an antidote to the cyber-information overload, with the motto "to seek the sacred in the ordinary".

The Old Biscuit Mill, 375 Albert Rd, Woodstock, 7925
www.clementina.co.za

ORANJEZICHT CITY FARM MARKET

CELEBRATION OF URBAN FARMING

The Oranjezicht City Farm Market Day is held every Saturday and Sunday, come rain or shine. The market is a cheerleader for local produce helping the artisanal culture to flourish in Cape Town. The market is home to a wide variety of locally-grown fresh produce, free-range meats and dairy, baked goods, wild-caught fish and seafood, cured meats, plants, flowers and homeware. There is a large variety of ready-to-eat or made-while-you-wait fresh, hot and cold foods to eat on-site. It is mostly outdoors with great views of the Atlantic Ocean; traders are located in marquees and customers sit under Bedouin tents that provide protection from the elements.

Granger Bay Blvd, V & A Waterfront, Cape Town, 8051
www.ozcf.co.za

EXPLORE

CAPE WINELANDS

Only 45 minutes from Cape Town lies another awesome attraction: the Cape Winelands (including Stellenbosch, Franschhoek, Paarl and other areas), a region famed not only for award-winning wine estates but also for its high concentration of luxury boutique hotels, art galleries and internationally-renowned fine-dining restaurants.

BABYLONSTOREN

WINE AND FRUIT FARM

Babylonstoren is a historic Cape Dutch farm dating back to 1692. This wine and food farm is one of the best-preserved farmyards in the Cape. Babylonstoren is famous for its romantic garden labyrinth, which is laid out over 3.5 hectares and divided into 15 sections: fruit, vegetables, berries, bees for pollination and so on. Sunny afternoons can be spent here, where couples play hide-and-seek, love birds forget the time, or families and friends enjoy a walk in the lush environment, discovering all sorts of fresh fruits. The farm restaurants and shop offer great quality, fresh farm food, homemade bread and tasteful souvenirs for loved ones at home.

Klapmuts Simondium Road, Franschhoek, 7646
www.babylonstoren.com

MAJEKA HOUSE

AWARDED DESIGN HOTEL

Majeka House is a five-star boutique hotel in Stellenbosch, awarded best design hotel by Condé Nast Johansens 2017. Twenty-three rooms, four room categories and a variety of experiences can be enjoyed. This luxury hotel serves small and larger groups. Whether a garden with a pool is the priority or the mountain view or tranquil luxury in a creative space for everyday living, the Majeka House has it all. The spa area offers a chance of unwinding and be pampered, where beauty therapists massage the stress out of every muscle. In the Makaron restaurant, palates are spoiled with the à la carte style menu. The focus here is to provide mouth-watering food in an elegant and comfortable environment.

26 Houtkapper St, Anesta, Stellenbosch, 7600
www.majekahouse.co.za

WATERKLOOF

FINE DINING WITH SPECTACULAR VIEWS

This restaurant is a shining star in South Africa's restaurant industry. In fact, it is Number One in the country (announced at the Eat Out Mercedes-Benz Restaurant Awards in November 2018). Waterkloof Wine Estate combines traditional cuisine with a modern French twist. The interior is classical, elegant and extends from the chic tasting lounge to the wine cellar. If overwhelmed by choice in the restaurant, trust the chef and accept the recommended Waterkloof wine that accompanies each dish on either the à la carte or degustation menu. No disappointment for sure. The emphasis lies on using only the freshest seasonal ingredients and a variety of rare herbs and vegetables, which are homegrown on the estate.

Sir Lowry's Pass Rd, Somerset West, Cape Town, 7130
www.waterkloofwines.co.za

GRAND PROVENCE

SOPHISITICATED WINE ESTATE

Located in the heart of Franschhoek, this wine farm with its dignified presence on the main road has thrived for over 300 years. The 18th century, grand, white manor house stands proudly in the middle of the estate. The restaurant and wine-tasting area of Grande Provence project a chic industrial presence. Steel joinery, galvanised metals and skylights distinguish this design approach. The wine-tasting area is next to the restaurant, where the bar dominates the centre of the room. Besides being chic and elegant, a touch of fun is evident with the tractor seat bar stools where award-winning vintages or modern wines can be sipped and swirled.

Main Rd, Franschhoek, 7690
www.grandeprovence.co.za

TOKARA

EXCEPTIONAL VINEYARD

The home of Tokara Wine Estate lies in the heart of the Cape Winelands at the foot of the Simonsberg Mountains. Award-winning wines can be enjoyed with dramatic views over Stellenbosch and False Bay. At the same time, the Tokara Deli and Restaurant offer modern South African cuisine and the opportunity to purchase delicacies such as olives, homemade jams and other delicious patés. The building housing the restaurant is a Cape architectural icon utilising glass, steel and stone. It includes a bar with a clear view of the hustle and bustle in the kitchen or the sun setting through a picture window.

Helshoogte Road (R310), Stellenbosch, 7600
www.tokararestaurant.co.za

JEWELL'S

FARM-TO-TABLE RESTAURANT

Liam Tomlin of the Chefs Warehouse Group and charcuterie master Neil Jewell previously of Bread & Wine joined forces in April 2019 to bring a farm-to-table restaurant to the Cape Winelands. Jewell's is an exquisite dining restaurant, located on the popular Spice Route destination near Paarl. While guests enjoy the beautiful view overlooking the mountains, the restaurant focuses strongly on cuisine that truly celebrates the produce of the Spice Route and surrounding farms. The wine list comprises a Spice Route selection, soon to include a new range of natural wines, produced here in clay vats imported from Georgia in Europe. And of course, Jewell's features Neil's famous charcuterie.

Spice Route Destination, Suid-Agter-Paarl Rd, Paarl, 7646
www.spiceroute.co.za/artisans/jewellsrestaurant

OVERTURE

PICTURESQUE WINELANDS RESTAURANT

The Hidden Valley wine estate is a gem waiting to be discovered on the slopes of the Helderberg Mountains. Not only does it have excellent wines and a spectacular location with breathtaking views over the vineyards and mountains of Stellenbosch, it also has an award-winning restaurant, Overture. Celebrated South African chef Bertus Basson and his team take their inspiration from old food memories and their mothers' recipes, and have regularly been awarded by the Eat Out Guide and Rossouw's Restaurant Guide. In Bertus' words: "We do not long for days gone by, but believe that traditional cooking is the foundation for our progressive South African cuisine".

Hidden Valley Wines, Annandale road, Stellenbosch
www.bertusbasson.com

THE WERF AT BOSCHENDAL

FARM TO TABLE DINING

Boschendal wine farm comprises the whole package: magical scenery, exquisite gardens, heritage, tranquillity and attention to detail. Situated in Franschhoek, the Werf Restaurant is located inside the beautifully revamped original cellar of the Boschendal Manor House. The focus lies on contemporary farm-to-table dining using the best available local, seasonal and ethically-sourced ingredients, serving exceptionally good and healthy food. Everything is sourced from the biodynamic garden next to the wine farm, so expect to see the chefs walking in the vegetable and herb garden to pick some fresh ingredients while preparing the meal.

Boschendal Estate, Pniel Road, Groot Drakenstein, Franschhoek, 7680
www.boschendal.com

NORVAL FOUNDATION

LARGE PRIVATE ART COLLECTION

Those who relish local art experiences within a lush garden should take a drive to the Norval Foundation in Steenberg. In addition to the landscaped sculpture garden, it offers nine gallery spaces as well as its spacious atrium, with yawning views of the adjacent Table Mountain National Park. The museum focuses on the research and exhibition of modern, contemporary art, showcasing the work of 20th- and 21st-century artists. It also combines art with an appreciation for nature. The Sculpture Garden, outdoor amphitheatre, purpose-built exhibition spaces and a research library provide a multisensory experience. The Norval Foundation also has a significant collection of books on South African art. This is complemented by the Skotnes Restaurant and Bar, a bespoke shop and a children's playground.

4 Steenberg Rd, Steenberg Estate, Cape Town, 7945
www.norvalfoundation.org

LA PETITE FERME

ROMANTIC COUNTRY-STYLE HOTEL

La Petite Ferme is both small and grand. Attention to detail is the motto here, this is why La Petite Ferme is popular among local and international guests.

Located in the Franschhoek Valley, a sensory overload is already created as the views always take the breath away. With exceptional cuisine, boutique wines and luxurious accommodation, La Petite Ferme is synonymous with the Franschhoek Valley. Just an hour's drive from Cape Town, tranquillity and luxury can be found here. The restaurant on the farm is surrounded by great scenery and offers a simple menu like cooked trout caught in La Petite's Ferme own dam. Sit back and relax while looking over the vineyards to the mountains.

Franschhoek Pass Road, Franschhoek, 7690
www.lapetiteferme.co.za

CHEFS WAREHOUSE
AT MAISON

SOPHISITICATED WINE ESTATE

Once upon a time, there was a chef who established three successful eateries in Cape Town. When the magnificent setting of the Maison Estate in Franschhoek came under consideration, Liam Tomlin decided to create yet another taste experience to match the breathtaking views of the estate. So, the award-winning tapas concept of the Chefs Warehouse brand came to the Cape Winelands. It is certainly recommended to drive out to Franschhoek despite the fact that there are two other Chefs Warehouse branches in Cape Town. The highlight here is the grilled hake: it's firm and flaky and is served with garlic bread to scoop up the sauce. Exclusive wines, each grape hand-selected, complement the dishes in an inviting way.

Maison Estate, R45, Franschhoek, Cape Town, 7690
www.maisonestate.co.za

LEEU ESTATE

LUXURY RETREAT

Set in and around enchanting Franschhoek, the Leeu Collection gives a new meaning to the concept of leisure. Leeu Estate is not only a luxury boutique hotel, spa and gym or wine estate, it is also a wonderland housing an extraordinary art collection and impressively landscaped gardens.

Luxurious and individually-styled bedrooms feature leather, wood and stone elements in a calm colour palette, while the dining room encourages afternoon tea or long meals savoured with fine wine from the cellar. The wellness sanctuary offers holistic treatments and the reading room at Leeu is an intimate space with a welcoming wood-burning fireplace. How can this combination not be irresistible?

Dassenberg Rd, Franschhoek, 7690
www.leeucollection.com

BOSJES

SOUTH AFRICAN FARM RESORT

BOSJES, meaning "small bushes" in Dutch, has been in the Botha/Stofberg family since 1831 and is now a working protea and fruit farm focused on playing a pivotal part in benefitting the community. Guests can enjoy the impressive landscape as well as the historical architecture along with the impressive modern additions. The farm features a charming boutique guesthouse, an open-air tea garden, and the BOSJES Kombuis restaurant. The highlight is the beautiful avant-garde chapel designed by Coetzee Steyn. It appears to rest lightly on the body of water before it and stands in the quiet space, looking out through the glass walls to the magnificence of the mountainous valley.

Bosjes, R43, Western Cape
www.bosjes.co.za

PATERNOSTER

Fishermen, fishing boats and bokkoms drying in the wind: Paternoster is one of the oldest fishing villages in the West Coast area. Even though travellers from all over are starting to explore this small town to take a break from the hectic city life, it is still a hidden gem that is worth discovering. With a splendid coastline, delicious cuisine – from simple restaurants serving seafood as fresh as can be to Kobus van der Merwe's iconic fine-dining restaurant "Wolfgat" – and the most charming guest houses and luxury boutique hotels, Paternoster definitely has something to offer to every traveller.

GAAITJIE

UNPRETENTIOUS AND MADE WITH LOVE

While this whitewashed fisherman's cottage tucked in among the rocks might seem simple from the outside, this gaaitjie ("small hole") has turned into a restaurant with spectacular views. Indeed, once inside, it is difficult to leave. The modest interior creates a familiar feeling of comfort. Rushing somewhere else after dinner is not possible or necessary here, as sustainable fresh local foods offer a memorable dining experience. All food is freshly cooked and the fish comes directly from the ocean. The wine list at Gaaitjie is vast and the focus is on wines from the West Coast.

Sampson St, Kliprug, Paternoster, 7381
www.gaaitjie.co.za

OEP VE KOEP

WEST COAST DELICACIES

Until recently, Kobus van der Merwe experimented in his bistro in his parents' gift shop, Oep ve Koep. There was no website and you had to go along the shelves with flowerhoney to a cosy garden with concrete benches and white tablecloths. Nevertheless, the culinary press manages to find him there. In recent years, Kobus has caused a sensation with his "strandveld tasting menus". "Strandveld" is the African name for the low vegetation of succulents and heather along the coast. Wherever we see some bushes, Van der Merwe sees a culinary treasure of vegetables and aromatic herbs.

St Augustine Rd, Paternoster, 7381
no website

STRANDLOPER OCEAN BOUTIQUE HOTEL

LUXURY OCEAN GETAWAY

Anyone looking for an unspoiled ocean getaway will feel perfectly at home at the Strandloper Ocean Boutique Hotel. Only 90 minutes from Cape Town, it offers exclusive accommodation, featuring comfortable and exquisite hotel rooms and suites with unforgettable views of the ocean. Looking after the environment, it offers eco-friendly appliances including solar heating and low energy air conditioners, while handmade rain bath products are in all suites and rooms. The use of natural cleaning products and materials emphasises Strandloper's motto "In harmony with nature". The hotel also strives to save water and energy. Everything with success: owls, bats, rodents and insects are attracted by the hotel and the vegetable garden is growing.

Patterson Slot, Paternoster, 7381
www.strandloperocean.com

WOLFGAT

PIONEER OF FORAGING FOOD

This pocket-sized restaurant was named best restaurant in the world at the prestigious 'World Restaurant Awards' in February 2019. Inspired by the West Coast landscape, with its dramatic seasonal transformation and unique Strandveld Fynbos plant kingdom, it satisfies fine dining cravings. All dishes are adapted according to the weather and the season. Chef Kobus van der Merwe decides the menu based on what can be found during the daily exploration of the coastline. Situated in a revamped fisherman's cottage in Paternoster, this intimate 20-seater eatery is committed to sustainable practices. All ingredients are locally sourced and foraged from Paternoster. Wolfgat is named after the nearby Wolfgat cave – an archaeological wonder containing remnants of an ancient culture.

10 Sampson Street, Paternoster, 7381
www.wolfgat.co.za

COPYRIGHT

© Travel Colours, 2019. All rights reserved. No part of this book may be copied, stored in a retrieval system, or transmitted in any form by any means, electronic, mechanical, recording or otherwise, except brief extracts for the purpose of review, and no part of this book may be sold or hired, without the written permission of the copyright owner.

. . .

The information in this Travel Colours Guide is checked regularly. Every effort has been made to ensure that this book is up-to-date as possible at the time of going to press. Although the authors have taken all reasonable care in preparing this book, we make no warranty about the accuracy or completeness of its content and, to the maximum extent permitted, disclaim all liability arising from its use.

. . .

Text Copyright © TravelColours, 2019
Photographs Copyright © TravelColours, 2019
(unless otherwise mentioned)

The publisher would like to thank the following for their kind permission to reproduce their photographs:

Erin Wulfsohn (@erinwulfsohn) for Pursch Artistes (@purschartistes) p.7, picture on the bottom; Tim Johnson p. 10; Cape View Clifton p. 14-17; Matthieu Joannon p. 18; The Royal Portfolio p. 20-21; Gorgeous George p. 22-25; La Grenadine p. 26-29; POD p. 30-33; Perfect Hideaways p. 34-37; Adriaan Louw p. 38-41; Herique Wilding Michel p. 42-45; Elsa Young/Frank Features p. 46-49; Hemelhuijs p. 52; Tyrone Bradley p. 58; MRKT p. 60; Live Bait p. 62; La Parada p. 64-67; The Yard p. 71; Andrea van der Spuy p. 88, 91; The Test Kitchen p. 94; FYN, Bruce Tuck p. 100-103; Salsify at the Roundhouse p. 110; The Athletic Club & Social p. 124; Tjing Tjing p. 126; Dear Rae p. 140; Maison Mara p. 142; Kate McLuckie p. 144; Chapel p. 146; Babylonstoren p. 158-161; Majeka p. 162; Tokara p. 170; Bosjes p. 200-203; Strandloper Ocean Boutique Hotel p. 210.

BERLIN

CAPE TOWN

MILAN

PALMA DE MALLORCA

PARIS

REYKJAVÍK

STOCKHOLM

TBILISI

AND MORE AVAILABLE AT

www.travelcolours.guide